Bridgtown and District Local History

THE HISTORY OF
BRIDGTOWN

Volume 2 - Bridgtown's Industrial Heritage
William Gilpin, Cornelius Whitehouse and others

David Williams

Published in 2018 by Bridgtown & District Local History Society

ISBN 978-1-9997666-3-4

Designed and produced by John Griffiths. Printed in England.

Contents

Foreword

Bridgtown & District Local History Society was formed in 2009. Since then it has published eight books based on the memories and reminiscences of its members and on the evidence it has been able to gather.

This book is one of a series of six new books which seek to outline the actual history of the village of Bridgtown. When put together these books tell the story of Bridgtown through history, starting even before the birth of the village in 1861 right through to the present day. The society has worked hard to gather as much accurate information as possible. However sometimes the only evidence available has come to us by word of mouth. We have tried to avoid any inaccuracies and to verify stories that have been reported to us.

I would like to place on record my thanks and appreciation to all the people who have provided information and photographs so that the history of this community can be charted before it all disappears into the sands of time. I would also like to express deep gratitude to those members of the society who have given up their time to write one of the books or part of a book. Contributors and writers have worked together with a common aim in true Bridgtown spirit. Thank you to all of them.

In addition, thank you to the Greenway Trust for sponsoring these books and to John Griffiths for his professional support and advice which has been invaluable. The author would also like to thank the late David Battersby both for his research and his inspiration. *"The History of Bridgtown"* will be written over a 3 year period with the final book appearing towards the end of 2020. As editor of the series I will be pleased to receive feedback from any reader during this period.

David Williams, October 2018

CONTACT INFORMATION

Joint Chairmen:	John Devey	01922 412008
	David Williams	01889 802534
Secretary:	Derrick Middleton	01543 277268
Membership:	Bob Brevitt	01922 414863
Email:	bridgtownhistory@hotmail.com	
Website:	http://www.bridgtownhistory.co.uk	

Chapter One: **Industrial Heritage**

The village of Bridgtown was created in 1861 by Wolverhampton Building Society who drew up plans for a new town and called it Bridgtown. Before then industry had come to the area in the form of the edge tool industry created by William Gilpin. Coal mining was also growing in importance and was developing apace. The new town was being built for the workers in these new industries so that they could live in good housing near to their employment.

Four families were mainly responsible for providing the new sources of employment for Bridgtown families. The family names were Gilpin, Whitehouse, Wootton and Hawkins. Although never actually living in Bridgtown himself, the man most responsible for the appearance of Bridgtown was William Gilpin. Some 70 years earlier he had set up a factory in Wedges Mills to make augers. At the beginning of the nineteenth century he had further developed his business at nearby Churchbridge so that he was making a variety of edge tools. Chapter Two will tell his story in full. Having initially built himself a new home, Forge House, in Wedges Mills, he later went on to establish a new family home called Longford House on the other side of Watling Street. Gilpin brought new skilled workers from other parts of the country and they had to have somewhere to live.

The Gilpin family home Longford House was built around 1800. Many extensions were built and the family lived there for just over a hundred years.

The Whitehouse family had an immense influence on the growth and development of Bridgtown. All the male members of this family had their initial employment at Gilpin's but then developed their own companies. They became residents themselves and deeply affected the community life of the village, being devout Methodists. There were two main edge tool companies set up by the Whitehouses, but both of these came after the birth of the village. The Whitehouse companies and stories are to be found in Chapter Four and Chapter Five.

Another family that were in at the very start of Bridgtown was the Wootton family. Abraham Wootton actually moved his business to Bridgtown in 1861 itself and built himself a large house on the corner of Park Street and North Street. Later his two sons developed his timber business further and themselves resided in the village. Their story is in Chapter Six.

This aerial photograph was taken in the late 1930s. By this time Wootton's Timber Yard was only used for storing large tree trunks left to season.

The Hawkins family actually came from nearby Cheslyn Hay but had a profound effect on Bridgtown by developing their tile works alongside Watling Street. Yet again this business grew out of the Gilpin empire at Churchbridge.

There was a factory in Walkmill Lane before 1861 and this was the only other existing industrial company to be around when Bridgtown was built. This company is a story of soap and fertiliser and also appears in Chapter 6.

This is a view of Hawkins Longhouse Tileries. It shows the original "marl hole" in the foreground.

Chapter Two:
William Gilpin Senior & Co. Ltd.

WE ACCLAIM THEIR MAJESTIES

MAY THEY REIGN

The edge tool business of Gilpin's preceded the birth of Bridgtown by some years. In that respect William Gilpin was the man most responsible for the birth of Bridgtown as a community. So who was William Gilpin? How did he come to live in the area and what was his background?

He was born in 1755 at the Red Cow Inn in Dudley Street, Wolverhampton. His father was Thomas Gilpin, who was a butcher as well as an innkeeper, and his mother was named Carolina. His parents were reasonably well-off and he will have received a reasonable education.

As a young teenager he was apprenticed to Daniel Fieldhouse, an auger maker with a smithy in Hollow Lane, now called Bell Street, in Wolverhampton. Fieldhouse was a heavy drinker who spent a lot of his time at the Red Cow Inn. Thomas Gilpin was aware that Fieldhouse was a very competent blacksmith and auger maker. On the strength of this he was happy to apprentice William to him in return for the debt owed to him by his customer.

Another of the regular customers in the Red Cow was a coal higgler called George Bradney, who was a person who purchased coal at the pit head and sold it to domestic customers. This coal was packaged in baskets called dassets and carried by horse around the countryside. In those days the condition of the roads was so bad that this was the only practical way of delivering coal to outlying areas. One day Bradney was upset by Mr. & Mrs. Gilpin who asked him to move away from the fireside in order to allow a "gentleman" access to the warmth. It is thought that this incident incensed George Bradney and gave him the self-motivation to work hard and become a "gentleman" in his own right. This incident also was to have an important effect on William Gilpin and, hence, on the birth of Bridgtown.

In those days in Wolverhampton edge tool makers were mainly blacksmiths, making shovels and axes. Augers were a more specialised tool. Daniel Fieldhouse was an auger maker whose products were destined for the dockyards as they were used in the construction of the timber ships of those days. Not surprisingly, Fieldhouse decided to move to London nearer to the dockyards, taking William with him. Ultimately William's role became an organiser of other people who worked for them. William also watched and learned from other craftsmen and studied the range of other edge tools and the uses to which they could be put. Once his apprenticeship was complete, he returned to Wolverhampton with a view to becoming his own master.

This is a photograph of a painting of William Gilpin as he was in later life. The painting was only rediscovered in 2014 after going missing for decades. William was nearly 80 when he died in 1834.

Now twenty-one, William initially had to be content with a little smithy among the pig pens at the rear of the Red Cow. Gradually William built up his clientele and eventually he employed Edward Smith as his assistant. Edward learned quickly and so William was able to move his business to London Row (now Piper's Row) in 1786. The tools were ground by means of a gin horse mill but already William's thoughts were turning to the acquisition of a water mill which would be so much more efficient. Eventually he expanded into a third hearth and employed a lad named Thomas Morgan.

Meanwhile George Bradney had worked hard and become a wealthy farmer who still visited the Red Cow on market days as the inn provided him with a suitable venue where he could conduct his business deals. Bradney had graduated from very small sales into larger purchases and sales. He had now progressed to renting out small farms, rearing his own cattle and growing crops at his own farm in Little Wenlock. Even Thomas Gilpin bought livestock from Bradney as the quality was good. George Bradney had indeed become a "gentleman".

It was the custom on market days for farmers to bring their wives with them but, as George Bradney's wife had died, he brought along his eldest daughter Jane. William agreed to meet Jane on behalf of one of the men who sold his augers for him but found himself entranced by the young lady. Jane and William contrived to meet again and began to do so quite regularly. George Bradney made it very clear that he did not approve of William Gilpin but this only seemed to strengthen the bond between the two.

William told Jane about the precarious nature of his business together with an explanation of why he found it difficult using a horse to grind his augers. He said he needed a water mill. Jane revealed that a few years earlier her father had purchased a mill on a brook called Blade's Mill near to Cannock. This mill had had a varied history having been both a corn mill and a mill used in the manufacture of agricultural tools. Originally the mill had been owned by two brothers named Wedge and it had been called Wedges' Mill. As yet her father had not decided what to do with it.

Even before this conversation William had decided to ask Bradney for Jane's hand in marriage, and now he rather hoped that she would arrive with Blade's Mill in the other hand! Bradney bluntly refused William's request without giving a reason so William asked Jane to marry him secretly. Jane made a further request to her father to no avail, so she then agreed to William's plan. After two court cases on the matter and with no dowry on offer, Jane and William were married at St. Peter's Church in Wolverhampton on a market day, namely 6th May 1784. At first George was furious and left them to struggle along on their own. Jane had been used to struggle in the days before her father had become wealthy and this did not seem to bother her. She remained on good terms with both her husband and her father. William and Jane's first child, George Bradney Gilpin, was born in March 1785. Only after this event did Jane make the request to her father for Blade's Mill as her home and the gift was not withheld. So it was that William Gilpin brought his edge tool business to the place which eventually was called Wedges Mills.

It still took some time for this to happen as it was 1790 or 1791 before his works completely moved there. Gilpin was suffering from lack of capital and the alterations were confined to putting up three or four hearths and erecting a house for the family. This house was called Forge House. By this time three further children had arrived, William Cecil in 1787, Catherine Bridget in 1788 and Jane Caroline in 1789. It must have taken some time to adapt the mill for auger grinding because once a week William used to load the augers into the paniers on his horse and take them to a grinding mill at Bentley. He used the same means of transport to take the finished orders to market in Birmingham.

Forge House in Wedges Mills was originally built for William Gilpin's family. Initially the house also had to be the home for his workers too. Later he moved his family to their new home of Longford House.

Gradually the business developed and the clack of Blade's Mill was heard again, but grinding iron not corn. Larger workshops were built as were small houses for employees just down the road. A small village developed around the factory and William no longer confined himself to making augers. Now he manufactured heavier edge tools.

These cottages in Wedges Mills were built to house William Gilpin's workers as his business grew. The three storey cottages were quite unique in that they were genuine "back to back" housing. Within the Cannock Chase area they were one of the last surviving examples of such housing until they were demolished in the 1950s.

One day he rode to Coaly in Gloucestershire and returned in triumph with Richard Newman who had worked at the Underwood works there. Richard was an ingenious toolmaker who fully understood the working of the new forge hammers at Coaly Mills. Soon there was a forge hammer at Blade's Mill and employment offered to many men to move there from Coaly Mills. Now Gilpin had a workforce experienced in making adzes, axes and ship's carpenters' tools. Soon it was possible to make even heavier edge tools.

There was only one further way in which Gilpin could increase his profitability and that was by finding cheaper coal and iron. At that time he obtained his coal from Essington Wood but he was sure that coal was to be found in nearby fields. Indeed coal was discovered there and this story is related at the beginning of Chapter Three.

Early in the nineteenth century William Gilpin bought some land at Churchbridge, on the junction of Watling Street and Walsall Road. There is significant evidence of edge tools being made there in 1817. However it is fairly certain that industry had started there as early as 1804, with definite proof of factory buildings being constructed in 1806.

Gilpin bought some land early in the nineteenth century and developed it significantly. Here is how it looked a hundred years later.

Now William wanted to strengthen his trade by manufacturing his own iron and steel. He purchased an eligible site opposite the coal wharf and soon had a flourishing mill for working iron and steel.

He went on making shell augers until 1820 but then changed to making twist augers as a result of information from his son George who had toured the country developing his knowledge.

By now William was an old man but he did not die until 30th August 1834 when he was almost 80 years of age. He died in Birmingham but he is buried at St. Luke's Church in Cannock.

For some time his second son William had been in charge of the works at Churchbridge and at Wedges Mills. Legends about the Gilpin family abound but they often confuse father and son who bore the same name, as the two not only looked alike but were similar in terms of character and drive. The company was now growing rapidly and in 1837 they built a chimney stack which was 180 feet high and could be seen from miles around. This was a local landmark and can be seen in the photograph above. It remained there until 1933 when it was demolished. For many years the works also housed a steam engine made by James Watt.

The very large chimney stack at Gilpins was demolished on 25th November 1933. Here are workers from the auger shop celebrating its demise by sitting on the rubble. Nevertheless a local landmark had been removed forever.

They put down rails to transport the coal, using iron tubs. They purchased whole trees to cut up for the handles of their tools. They took a hundred tons of coal daily from the nearby Great Wyrley Colliery Company. They worked night and day to produce iron from the puddling furnaces and rolling mills. They produced both iron and steel and the site had a number of bottle kilns for this purpose. By 1850 the Gilpins were mine owners, iron & steel makers, axle makers and edge tool makers. They were in the right place at the right time to join in England's total dominance in supplying the world with metal goods.

The works was in an ideal position for transport links. Although positioned perfectly alongside the main roads of Watling Street and Walsall Road, it was the railway and canal links that were even more important. The company had its own sidings linked to the Birmingham – Rugeley railway line which had been constructed during the 1850s and the canal links were an even greater advantage. The thirteen locks between Churchbridge and Leacroft were officially opened in 1860, linking the Staffordshire Worcester Canal with the Birmingham Canal Navigation.

The thirteen locks between Churchbridge and Leacroft linked the Staffordshire and Worcester Canal with the Birmingham Canal Navigation. Gilpin's Works was ideally placed to use this connection.

Other edge tool manufacturing companies were also moving into the area and Wolverhampton Building Society had the forethought to plan a new town close to these successful businesses. So it was that Bridgtown grew rapidly during the 1860s and the 1870s, being home for many of the expanding workforce at Gilpin's Churchbridge base.

It was the time of the early Exhibitions and Gilpin's won the silver medal at the "Exposition Universelle de 1867 a Paris". They won the bronze medal at the International Exhibition Sydney N.S.W. 1879. They were overjoyed to win the gold medal at the International Exhibition

This photograph shows some of the international medals that Gilpin's won at exhibitions held all around the world.

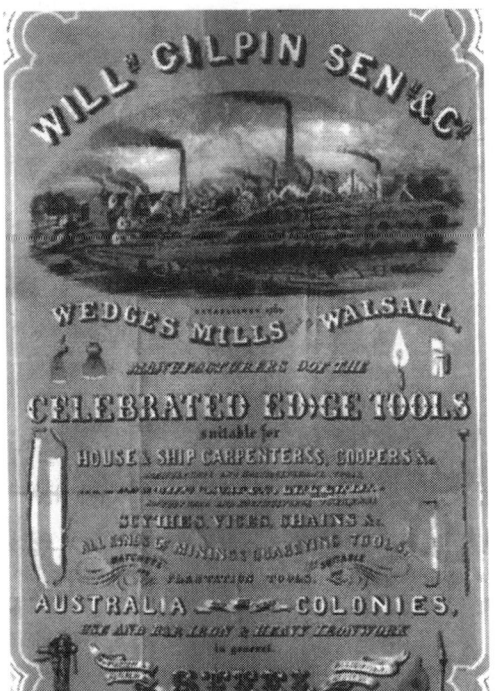

This is a page from a nineteenth century Gilpin's catalogue. Note the addresses. The factory at Wedges Mills was still in existence. Their other address was given as Near Walsall because Bridgtown did not exist.

Melbourne 1880 as well as another bronze medal at the South African International Exhibition Kimberley 1892. These were years of full order books and intense activity at Churchbridge.

Gilpin's had become a well-known worldwide company. This was mainly through the ability and enterprise of Frederick Gilpin who ran the company at this time. He travelled the world searching out new outlets for their products such as sugar cane knives and hoes of every description. The items they made were an encyclopaedia of modern tools. They seemed to make everything.

On the main Walsall Road stood the Robin Hood public house. This too was owned by Gilpin's and was a popular hostelry. The men who worked at Gilpin's worked very hard but they were glad to do so. They believed in their company and were proud to work there. However, they did not frequent the Robin Hood as they had their own public house, not surprisingly called The Red Cow. This stood in the company grounds and was the middle one of a set of three terraced cottages. Beer at the Red Cow was one penny a pint. There was also a "tummy shop" where food was bought without ready money. Tokens were issued with the goodwill of the firm and these were used for money until such time as the workman could pay.

Frederick Elphinstone Gilpin and his Argentinian wife, Mercedes R de Gilpin. Frederick moved to Argentina in the late nineteenth century, promoting the Gilpin company and its products.

The workforce were comrades with their own set of values. Later one of their number, Percy Sides, described them as "a band of men from whom to learn how to live and to acquire a set of values with which to meet all that the world had to fling – the most humorous, the most generous and friendly people the world over".

Gilpin's traditonally had a loyal band of employees. Each man on this photograph had completed fifty years of working for the company. Percy Sides is shown top left.

As the twentieth century began the world changed with periods of strife, war and competition from new and mighty nations. Nevertheless, Gilpin's continued to flourish as their catalogue of "modern" tools illustrated. It seemed as if they made everything.

This photograph shows some of Gilpin workers in 1913.The young lad seated at the front reminds us of the early age at which boys began to work in those days.

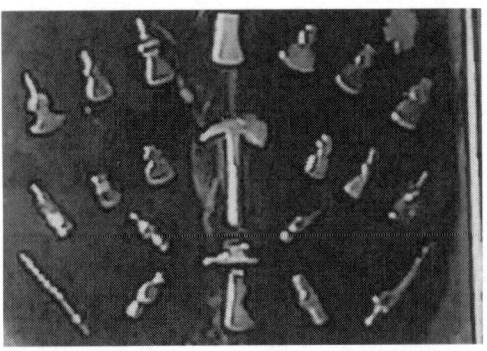

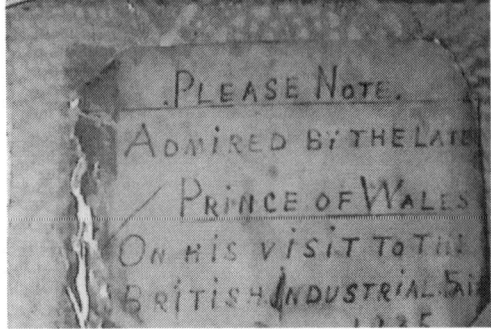

This photograph shows a display of tools at another event following the 1935 British Industrial Fair.

They made axles and axes, picks and shovels, hammers of every shape and weight, horseshoes for the British Army, vices for the British Navy, augers and brace bits, chisels for wood and steel, machine gun parts, rowlocks for boats and they were famous for

ESTABLISHED 1790.

W.GILPIN. WEDGES MILLS. W.G.

Churchbridge Works and Wedges Mills,
Cannock, Staffordshire.

Date 14th July 1922.

Telephone No. 7 Cannock.

Messrs J. G. Banfield & Sons, Ltd.,
Tenbury.

BOUGHT OF
WILLIAM GILPIN SENR. & Co., Ltd.

Order No. 29/5/22.

	21/-	23/- 25/6 doz.				
1½ doz. Hooks (Tenbury) ea.	10.	11. 12"		5. 4. 3		
		Plus 75%		3 18. 2.		9. 2. 5.
	18/-	18/- doz.				
1 doz. Scotch Bits ea.	5/16.	7/16"		1 16. 6.		
½ doz. " " ⅜"	18/-			13. 6.		
				2. 9. 6.		
		10%		4. 11.		2. 4. 7.
Per L. & N. W. Ry.			Case			2. 6.
						11. 9. 6.
		Allowance for Carriage				7. 6.
						11. 2. 0.

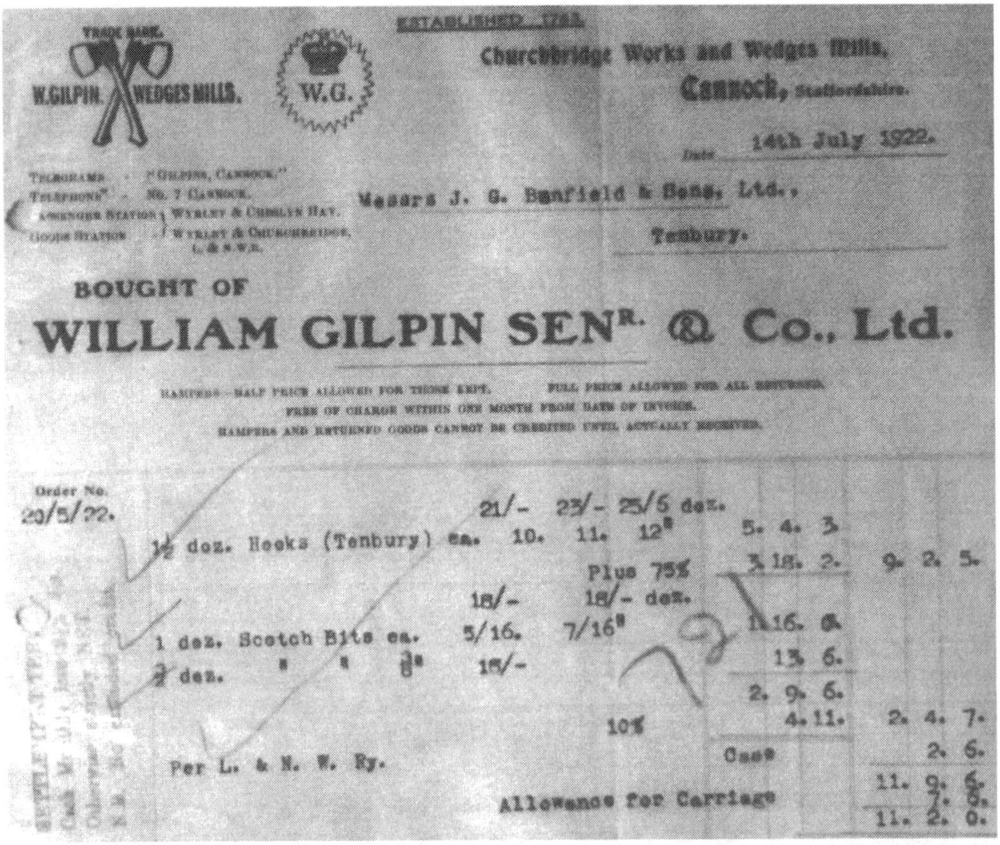

The 1922 invoice has an interesting telephone number. It really does say No. 7 Cannock. Note that the items were sent by the London & North West Railway, showing just how useful was the company's direct access to the local Birmingham to Rugeley line.

quoits. They had a worldwide reputation for cart and wagon axles, axles for street pianos, axles for rickshaws for China and Japan, machetes for Argentina, sugar cane knives for Cuba, hoes of endless varieties, marline spikes for the shipyards, sailors' needles for the repair of sails and much, much more!

An interesting feature was that certain tools seemed to be made by certain families. The Walker family made horseshoes. The Cartwright family made vices. The Corfield family made smaller axles while the Pursehouse and Thomas families made the heavy ones. The Sambrook family were markedly skilled and made all the tools for stamping and forging. Few of these men could read or write but they could make themselves clearly understood in the local vernacular dialect. They even designed the tools that made the tools they sold.

The recently amalgamated workforce of Gilpin & Whitehouse are pictured celebrating the coronations of King George VI and Queen Elizabeth in 1937.

However, the world continued to change and there was no longer the drive and enthusiasm of the early Gilpin family members. The successful years of Gilpin's waned and in the mid 1930s the company amalgamated with Whitehouse Bros. Ltd. of Bridgtown, as described in Chapter Five. Initially this provided more impetus for a short while only.

The Minister for Fuel & Power, Peter Thorneycroft (Left), is seen talking to Graham Mucklow in the late 1940s.

The company still had breath for one final fling and, in 1943, that company sold it to one Harry Mucklow. Rather like the original owner he was possessed of Midland engineering skill and drive. He soon licked it into shape and knocked the sleep out of it. His family business was Mucklow Bros. Ltd. of Blackheath in Birmingham. Harry Mucklow and his son Graham found time to pilot Gilpin's into a new trade of drop-forging and to link this with a considerable edge tool production. Yet again the company became successful.

Here are the auger shop workers in the days of Mucklow Bros. Ltd. Many of them have carried their tongues with them for the photograph.

Gilpin's tools were always popular and were well used both in England and abroad, even many years after the halcyon days of the exhibition successes of the nineteenth century. Many of their workforce continued to live in the adjacent communities of Bridgtown and Churchbridge well into the twentieth century.

This photograph shows a section of the Forging Shop and the tool being made is an auger. These were certainly days of the craftsman. No mass production in those days.

The larger photograph shows the assembly department for garden shears and the smaller photograph the Hot Press Forging and Drop Stamp Department. These were the days when manufacturing industries were the lifeblood of the British economy.

Gilpin's was always a family run business which cared for its workers who, in turn, showed the company great loyalty. Workers were encouraged to take part in sporting activities in the little spare time they had. The company even provided its own bowling green as shown in the photograph on page 22.

The end of the company finally came in August 1985. A company statement said that 22 workers had already left and that the remaining 35 would lose their jobs at the end of the month. The company had been crippled by "a drastic cutback in orders" and "a general decline in the hand tool industry". Talks had been held with Transport and General Workers' officials and that plant and machinery had been sold to Sheffield hand tool manufacturers Burgon & Ball. Two management staff had been transferred to the company's sister plant in Halesowen. Company Secretary Mr Kenneth Peters said "It is very sad as the company was founded in 1763 and has been operating on this particular site for well over a hundred years."

Bowls was a popular pastime and the green was well used. In the background can be seen LMS trucks in Gilpin's goods yard. Across the road was the famous White Lion Hotel. This is probably a 1930s photograph.

Footnote

It is interesting that the year 1763 was always quoted by the company as its start date. The date was emblazoned on the gates to their premises and always appeared on their invoices. Yet in 1763 William Gilpin was only eight years old. It is presumed that Daniel Fieldhouse had begun his business in that year and that the first William Gilpin had seen his business dealings as an extension and development of that original auger-making business.

Acknowledgement - Most of the research for this chapter was carried out by David Battersby, with help from Derrick Middleton, Katherine Page and John Devey.

Chapter Three: **Coal Mining**

The village of Bridgtown never actually contained a coal mine, although many Bridgtown men have worked as miners. The village was surrounded by other mines and the coal produced there was essential to the local edge tool industry.

It is, however, necessary to consider the area before Bridgtown was actually built. The first recorded coal mines seem to date back to about 1805. This was the time when one of William Gilpin's sons started to search for coal locally following the building of a new works at Churchbridge in 1803. This son was probably George who didn't take an active part in tool manufacturing himself, as his role seemed to have been to discover and supply the raw materials of coal, iron and wood.

Some of the first mines were sunk on the land which is currently occupied by the Toll Road and probably extended beneath the railway line and across towards Walk Mill Lane. These would not have been deep pits and the shafts would have been no more than 8 feet in diameter. There would have been one shaft per pit, but the shaft bottoms were almost certainly inter-connected to form a ventilation system. There may even have been drift mines in those spots where the seams of coal were closer to the surface.

The coal would have been transported on a tramway to the works as the railway was not built until 1859. At about the same time a coal shaft was sunk off Walkmill Lane on the site now occupied by Vine Court and Lakeside Boulevard. Apparently, it was

Many local men worked in the mines. This photograph shows young miners on their first day at work at Mid Cannock Colliery. Today, all the boys in this picture would still be at school.

said to be known as Walkmill Pit but it does not seem to have ever been worked. Old Ordinance Survey maps show no sign of a pit or of any spoil heaps.

In 1823 the first Lord Hatherton, who was already active in coal mining, had to close down pits that he had sunk on the Lichfield Road in Cannock, on the site of the current Asda store. This followed a dispute with Lord Anglesey over mineral rights. Lord Hatherton then looked at land owned by his mother, Mrs. Morton Walhouse, which ran along Watling Street from the Longhouse (the inn which used to stand where B&Q is now situated) to Wedges Mills. This site is now occupied by Finning (U.K.) and Linkway Retail Park. On the old tithe map it was shown as Asher's Bog. Drilling took place but no coal of any importance had been found at a depth of 90 yards. Later further boring was instituted by a Mr. John Gilpin under the superintendence of a Mr. Phillip Baker of Great Wyrley, a ground bailiff, to a depth of 842 feet. Shafts were then sunk to 90 yards and a seam of coal was worked. This seam was 7 feet in thickness and was called "Bottom Robins" by the miners. This colliery was named Waterloo Colliery to celebrate the Duke of Wellington's victory. The mine was worked for some time but it was later renamed as Longhouse Colliery.

In 1847 Joseph Palmer of Rugeley, father of the famous "Palmer the Poisoner", was working the Hayes Pit at Brereton for the Marquis of Anglesey but, because the mining figures were poor, his lease was terminated. Instead he was offered the Longhouse Pit which he worked for a little while until it closed in 1855, several years before the birth of Bridgtown as a community. This really saw the end of mining in the actual Bridgtown area and this site then took on another role which will be told elsewhere in this book.

This photograph of the Old Coppice Colliery was taken very early in the twentieth century. This mine was often referred to locally as Hawkins Colliery.

Bridgtown began to be built in the early 1860s. The houses were built to serve local industry and the first villagers were the families of men who worked locally. There were edge tool workers from Gilpin's at Churchbridge, there were men who worked at the new timber yard belonging to the Wootton family, there were workers from the new expanding Patent Urban Manure Company in Walkmill Lane and there were many coal miners. The miners worked at a variety of local pits such as Landywood, Wyrley Bank, Coppice Lane and Old Falls. Lots of new shafts had been sunk and the Wyrley and Essington Canal linked to The Nook colliery. At this time there was an influx of miners and clay workers from Shropshire.

In 1871 the Leacroft Colliery Company was founded on the site of Leacroft Hall. This followed the purchase of mineral rights from the hall's owner Mr. Gibbons who also received royalty payments of one shilling per ton once mining had begun. Preparations for the mine began including the sinking of shafts. Actual mining did not begin until 1874. This meant more jobs and more people moved into Bridgtown. By this time the initial building of the "Bridgtown Triangle" was nearly completed. The triangle was the common name for the area shown on the original plan. Most new miners for Leacroft Colliery would walk to work along Green Lane, although a few would walk alongside the flight of canal locks from Churchbridge up to Leacroft.

Walking to work was the only option in those days and explains why workers moved to Bridgtown, to be as near as possible to where they worked. However, there is evidence of people walking much greater distances every day. For example, there is evidence of a miner walking from Bridgtown to the new colliery at Huntington when it opened. This meant a walk of approximately 4 miles before and after a heavy shift and, in those days, they worked for 6 days every week!

Mid Cannock Colliery. This mine had a very unstable existence in its early days. It closed down twice and did not function effectively until the days of World War One.

The Mid Cannock Colliery Company was formed in 1873 but no shafts were sunk until 1876.Then, the mining started straight away. It is thought that there was a shortage of working capital. Unfortunately, this was a time of poor coal sales and in February 1880 they found it necessary to reduce the price of coal by two shillings per ton. The company were unable to maintain their deferred payments and went into voluntary liquidation soon afterwards.

In the following year a new Mid Cannock Colliery Company was formed with a share issue of £40,000. Drawing coal re-started in 1882 but these were difficult times for the coal industry. Mining was in the doldrums and this particular venture was underfunded. Unsurprisingly, the colliery was forced to close for a second time in 1884. This time the pit was totally abandoned on the surface and underground the workings and shafts were allowed to fill with water.

This view of Mid Cannock Colliery as it was seen by most people from Walsall Road through most of the twentieth century.

This photograph was probably taken in 1913 when workmen were building the new bridge for the railway line to Mid Cannock Colliery after William Harrison's takeover.

In 1913 the site was purchased for £45,000 by William Harrison who was a noted coal owner with business interests in Brownhills and Great Wyrley. Work started to re-open the pit in September of that year. By this time the pit shafts were entirely filled with water and the site completely overgrown. After 29 years it was a mammoth task to pump out the shafts and to erect winding houses and a boiler house. However, the work must have gone well because coal was being drawn up the shafts again by August 1914. The First World War was about to begin and these turned out to be very hard times for coalminers. Although they received good wages for those times there were not enough men to meet the demands of their work. Many Cannock Chase miners had left to serve in the war, particularly the tunnelers to work in the trenches, a thankless task that left them with numerous health issues as a consequence.

Mid Cannock Colliery stood adjacent to the railway line from Birmingham to Rugeley, a perfect position for transporting the coal. Here a steam train pulls away with the mine in the background.

In 1915 there was an explosion at Mid Cannock and this resulted in the deaths of five men but the mine quickly returned to normal working practices. In those days many of the miners were only teenagers.

When the war was over there was much less demand for coal than there had been during the war years. In the 1920s a plant was built at Leacroft Colliery to distil petrol from coal but this venture was not a success and closed down for lack of funds in 1929. In 1933 the plant was re-opened and was more successful second time around. The plant was able to produce 30,000 gallons of fuel per day using 150 tons of coal. However, the plant did not function for very long and then it closed down for good. These were the days when fuel bought from America and the Middle East was very cheap in comparison to the cost of coal. Running costs for the plant would have been substantial too. It is thought that this was probably the largest ever attempt in the United Kingdom to manufacture petrol from anything else other than from crude oil.

Leacroft Colliery continued to be very old-fashioned in its working practices. It employed over a hundred horses underground and there was no electricity until during the Second World War, but it continued to function independently until 1954. That year marked the end for coal being wound up the Leacroft shaft. However, underground connections had been made with Mid Cannock Colliery and coal extraction went in that direction. Leacroft shafts continued to be used for men and materials until 1963. Even then the shafts were kept open in order to pump out the water to keep neighbouring pits dry.

After its initial problems Mid Cannock Colliery illustrates a much more positive tale. Nevertheless, mining remained a hard and dangerous occupation. However, the colliery became a larger, more modern success story. The photograph on the next page shows the top of the mine shaft in the 1930s. In the 1920s new screens had been built and in 1933 pit baths were provided for the first time. A few years later, in 1942, a pit canteen followed. This was the first in the Cannock Chase area and was funded by the Miners Welfare Committee. The old ways had changed. No longer did miners set out for work with their "snap tins" (lunch boxes) and return home in their "pit black"! Several mines were now combined into one business called Cannock Associated Collieries Limited and brand new offices were built on the

Another view of Mid Cannock Colliery.

Walsall Road, close to Mid Cannock. The accompanying photograph shows these offices which were officially opened by the then Duke of Kent in 1942.

Here are the distinctive grand offices of Cannock Associated Collieries Ltd. However, coal mining on Cannock Chase had a limited life. Around 1960 the building was sold to Staffordshire County Council to be used for a variety of educational purposes. The twenty first century brought demolition and the end of an iconic building.

Coal was now mined using coal cutters and moved away from the coal face on conveyor belts. These in turn emptied the coal into tubs which were then brought up to ground level. The company looked after the miners and built houses for them to live in. Mid Cannock Colliery provided 130 such houses during the 1930s. Yet again another World War put the mines under intense pressure to produce as much coal as possible. The end of the war saw a new government in power with a policy of nationalisation. The coal industry came under the control of the National Coal Board. All mines, including Mid Cannock, were then brought up to national standards, with working conditions and safety paramount.

This photograph shows the top of the mine shaft at Mid Cannock Colliery.

Also, at that time, large numbers of Eastern European men came to work in Britain. They had been displaced by border changes and by Russia taking control in many Eastern European countries. These men were housed in a "miners' hostel" built on land off Walsall Road, on the Bridgtown side of Ridings Brook, the stream known locally as Jellyman's Brook. The men were housed in long Nissen Huts. There were about twenty men in each hut, each having a bed and a locker. Canteens were provided as were showers and leisure rooms. This hostel remained in place until the late 1950s.

In 1952 the mine installed electric winding gear, the work being carried out over an August bank holiday weekend. In the run-up to the change preparatory work had to be carried out. This involved the removal of the baffle from the steam exhaust. With the removal of the baffle the sound made by the steam exhaust was excruciatingly loud. People who heard it said that it was extremely loud, even a mile away. It sounded even worse at night.

During the 1950s Mid Cannock was an extremely productive mine, producing over 500,000 tons of coal. The "glory days" could not last of course and the danger signs began to emerge after an underground connection was made to the Huntington pit about 4 miles away. The end came in 1965. Yet again, the shaft was kept open in order to pump out underground water. This went on for a few years until the walls of the shaft began to deteriorate, probably because of the close proximity of Opencast Mining. It became necessary to make a new large borehole, wide enough to lower down a pump which was then used to extract the water.

There were other coalmines very near to Bridgtown. In 1851 there was a coal master by the name of Edward Sayer who was working two pits in Cheslyn Hay. One was the Old Falls Colliery and the other Coppice Colliery. The latter became the Old Coppice Colliery and was later known as Hawkins Colliery. It was very close to Bridgtown and was worked from 1875 until 1960. Joseph Hawkins worked for Sayer and it would appear that he took over the pits from Sayer as, by 1869, they were clearly being run by Joseph. Hawkins did not hold on to the Old Falls Colliery for long as we know that it was being worked by Bagnall & Sons in the early 1870s.

Hawkins Colliery originally had three shafts, one of which was used for ventilation. In later years one of the shafts was enlarged to be twelve feet in diameter. At this point the ventilation shaft went out of use and was covered over. This coincided with the reorganisation of the underground workings. All coal was transported by canal barge and by a two foot gauge tramway which went round the south side of the nearby reservoir and underneath the main railway line to the Churchbridge basin and rail sidings. This tramway was in use until round about the end of the nineteenth century. The company tried very hard to establish a

Workers and tubs at the bottom in the Old Coppice Colliery.

proper main line connection to the railway line at Cheslyn Hay. The company did succeed in purchasing the old Walkmill Flour Mill and, for a while, it was home for the manager of their brickworks which stood to the rear of the colliery.

These are the office buildings at the Old Coppice Colliery. It is interesting that attached to the offices are cottages where some of the employees lived.

31

When a railway was eventually constructed it ran from the brickworks through the screens across Lodge Lane, alongside of the canal loading basin and curved across Walkmill Lane across the site of the old mill. Here the land had been raised from the stream and canal level up to road level. The railway then went along the north-east side of the reservoir where it was practically on the border with Bridgtown. When it reached the main railway line the embankment was dug away and a timber viaduct was built to carry the main line. The Hawkins line then followed a very tight curve under the new bridge and ran parallel with the main line, crossing Station Road at the side of the railway bridge, after which it rose up to meet the main line at the Plant Pit Sidings.

Trucks loaded with coal leaving Old Coppice Colliery.

During its lifetime the colliery had three locomotives. Everyone called the first one "Sons" but its real name was Emlyn, It was an 0-6-0 locomotive made by the Lilleshall Company of Oakengates and delivered in 1880. The second was made by Peckett & Sons of Bristol and was called simply Hawkins. The final one was very powerful and was called Tony. It had been built by Hawthorne Leslie & Co in Newcastle on Tyne but was bought second-hand from George Cohen of Newcastle in 1927. Hawkins and Tony continued to work until the mine closed in 1960.

Hawkins Colliery was not a large pit by any means. In 1932 there were 976 men employed there. Both shafts were always dry due to the thick layer of clay in the area, but it was still necessary to pump out 26,000 gallons of water in any 24 hour period.

Mine ventilation was provided by fan from Bumstead & Chandler of Hednesford. All coal was cut and loaded by hand. There were no cutters or conveyor belts. They used 87 ponies underground and a further eight on the surface.

The company was unique in that it had an associated brick making plant which was powered by three electric motors. There were fourteen kilns altogether which turned out 56,000 bricks in a 24 hour period.

Taken in 1951, this photograph shows the shaker machine at Hawkins Colliery as the men called it.

Many houses in the Bridgtown and Cheslyn Hay areas were built with these bricks. More information about this tile making can be found in Chapter Six.

The owner of the Old Coppice Colliery Joseph Hawkins in a photograph taken later in life.

Joseph Hawkins passed away on 8th January 1907 at the grand old age of 95. He died at the family home which still stands to this day, "Ivy House" at the junction of High Street and Low Street in Cheslyn Hay. After his death the company was run by his sons and by his grandsons right through till the time of nationalisation at the beginning of 1947. At this time the chairman and managing director was Major Osmond Crutchley Hawkins and there was a workforce of eight hundred men. Nationalisation brought many changes to all coalmines but spelt the end for Hawkins Colliery. The last coal left the canal basin for Stourport Power Station in 1949 but it was another ten years before its official closure was announced in the local press on 12th November 1959. All 300 employees were offered alternative employment elsewhere or a sum of £500 if they were leaving the industry. The last shift finished work on Good Friday, 15th April 1960.

Bridgtown still retained links with the coal industry for many years, however, as opencast mining was to appear right on its doorstep at neighbouring Churchbridge. More of this can be found in Volume 5 of this series.

Acknowledgement - Most of the research for this chapter was carried out by Katherine Page, with help from Mick Drury and Cheslyn Hay & District Local History Society.

Chapter Four:
Cornelius Whitehouse & Sons Ltd.

Gilpin's was the first edge tool company in the area but others were to follow. Job Whitehouse worked for Gilpin's and lived with his wife Elizabeth in the home of William Cecil Gilpin, William Gilpin's second son. Job's eldest son, Cornelius, was born there on 14th January 1825, but when their second son Isaiah was born they moved to a small house, one up and one down, in a row nearby. At three and a half years, Cornelius started school under the tutelage of a Mr. Henshaw but in 1831 he moved to the National School in Cannock.

In 1833 Job moved his family to Wolverhampton to work for a Mr. John Parsons. This was because Gilpin's had given him a cut in wages. One day Cornelius was taking his father's breakfast to him at the works. Cornelius ventured on to the platform of the forge engine and unfortunately suffered an accident while there. Only the speedy action of the engineer saved the boy but still two of his fingers were badly damaged. For the rest of his life, whenever attention was drawn to his scars and his injuries, Cornelius would say that he had been "miraculously saved for better things".

The photograph shows the premises of Cornelius Whitehouse & Sons Ltd. as they were in the 1940s.

In 1834 Job returned to work for Gilpin's and the family now settled in Cheslyn Hay. When Cornelius was nine years old, his father would take him to work before he went to school and his job was to start the forge hammer by opening a gate. This released water which in turn determined the speed of the hammer. Job had a hearth where he made drawing knives and socket chisels. When Cornelius became sixteen he went permanently to work with his father. A few years later Job took on a second hearth where his younger son Isaiah worked. Cornelius completed his apprenticeship by going to work for Thomas Morgan at Gilpin's. By now Morgan's eyesight was failing and he allowed his young striker to do nearly all of the work.

At twenty-one years of age Cornelius married Emma Goodfellow in March 1846 and they moved into the cottage in Wedges Mills where Cornelius had lived previously. Some-time later his brother Isaiah married Emma's sister Jane. Before the end of 1846 Emma gave birth to a son who they named Handel and, in 1850, they had a second son called Haydn. These two names reflected Cornelius's great love for music. After a while the family moved to Cheslyn Hay and then moved again to Bridgtown in 1863. Whenever they moved, Isaiah and Jane moved too to be their next door neighbours.

When he formed his own company, Cornelius chose a hedgehog for the company's trademark, presumably emphasising the sharpness of his edge tools. Here are photographs of two examples as they actually appeared on their products. Unfortunately they are a little worn with age.

Cornelius had a bright and innovative brain and was always researching and experimenting with new approaches to his work. He made a number of changes to production methods which made him very unpopular with the other employees. He invented his "patent mill bill" which had movable steelings. He sold it to Gilpin's for £50 but they suppressed it as it would have meant reducing prices.

A short time later he invented his first auger. A court case ensued in order to resolve the rights of ownership. It was agreed that in the United Kingdom the patent would belong to Gilpin's and for that they had to pay Cornelius £50. The patent for the rest of the world however was awarded to Cornelius himself. Eventually he sold the patent and manufacturing rights to another company for £150.

By 1868, at the age of 43, Cornelius had established an edge tool manufacturing company of his own on Walsall Road, Bridgtown. This was funded by the sale of the patents from his inventions. He was joined in this venture by his two sons Handel, now aged 21, and Haydn, now 18. So it was that the business "Cornelius Whitehouse & Sons" came into being and Cornelius began to justify his belief that he was "saved for better things". His younger brother Isaiah also left Gilpin's to join in the new venture. In the 1871 census Cornelius was said to employ "four men and three boys"

Cornelius's father Job had been a profound influence on his early life and had engendered his imaginative approach to work. Job however continued to work for Gilpin's and did so for 60 years, apart from that short spell in 1833. Job died in 1883, aged 80 years. All his life Cornelius had enjoyed a close working relationship and friendship with his brother Isaiah who himself died in November 1886.

The new business started to produce a very wide range of edge tools, supplying the needs of the home, of small businesses and of large employers. Handel and Haydn began to play a very important role in developing the company further, particularly by serving markets outside the United Kingdom. This is illustrated by the extremely successful trip to Australia and New Zealand undertaken by Haydn in the early 1890s.

Cornelius Whitehouse.

Here is a happy group of female workers at the factory in 1925.

When his wife Emma died on 2nd May 1896 at the age of 69 and after 50 years of marriage, Cornelius decided to retire. He passed control of the business to his sons. He himself died on Thursday 23rd March 1899, aged 74 years. He had risen from very humble beginnings to be his own master. Nowadays he is very fondly remembered for his love of music and for the many tunes and hymns that he wrote. Some of these are still sung today, particularly by local choirs and church congregations.

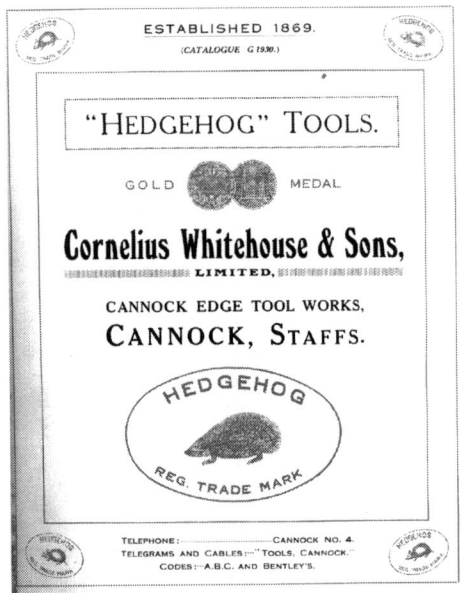

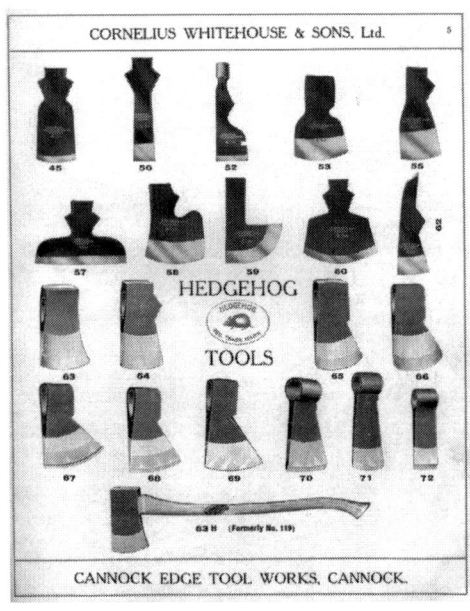

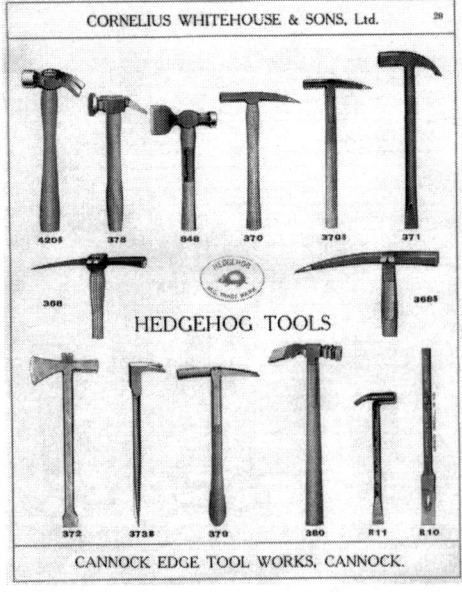

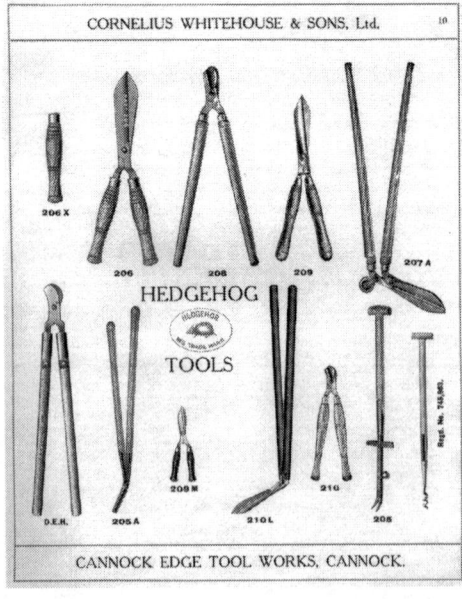

The title page and three product pages taken from the company's 1930 catalogue showing a small selection of their vast range of tools. Note the telephone number.....Cannock 4.

Handel Whitehouse married Ann Wood in 1871 and they had nine children. They had six girls, two of whom died in infancy, and three boys. The boys' were named Julian Osborn born in 1876, George Milton, born in 1881, and Norman Frank, born in 1884. Handel was appointed as managing director on the retirement of his father and he continued the growth and development of the company. Unfortunately, Ann died in November 1892 but Handel remarried in July 1893. His new wife was Mary Charles, a widow aged 34. Handel himself died in 1903 at The Woodlands, Walsall Road, Bridgtown, aged 56. He left his share of the business to his son Julian. In the 1911 census both George and Norman and all four of their sisters were still living at The Woodlands. Both George and Norman gave their occupation as Edge Tool Manufacturers and Employers.

This is the Trip Hammer Forge at the factory.

Haydn Whitehouse had also worked for Gilpin's prior to the establishment of the family business. He played an extremely important part in the growth of the company. He married Fanny Smith in 1877 and they had 14 children in 18 years, eleven of which were girls. The three boys were Reginald, born in 1885, Oswald, born in 1888 and Cyril, born in 1896. Sadly, Cyril was killed almost at the end of World War One on 24th May 1918 at Arras, Pas-de-Calais. He was 21 years old.

These photographs show both sides of the gold medal won by the company at the International Trade Exhibition in New Zealand in 1906-07.

Haydn had become managing director on the death of his brother in 1903. He was supported by his nephew Julian, then aged 27. Further family support came from his own son Reginald, then aged 18, and his nephews George, then 22, and Norman, then aged 19. Haydn's other son Oswald joined the company later after completing his education. Haydn's wife Fanny died in 1927 and two years later he decided to retire. He left the area and settled in Blackpool where he died in 1941 at the good age of 90 years.

Throughout the 1930s and the 1940s the business continued to grow and thrive under the continued management of the Whitehouse family. Julian had been appointed as managing director on the retirement of Haydn and he was knighted for his services to the community. He had married Florence Gallatley in 1900 and they had three

sons, Frederick (1902), Eric (1904) and Ernest (1910), all listed as Edge Tool Manufacturers. When Julian died at his home, 84 Hatherton Road Cannock, he left his shares in the company equally to his three sons.

Reginald Whitehouse had been a very strong driving-force in the company for some time and he took

Here Reginald Whitehouse is on the right. He was Managing Director during World War Two.

over as Managing Director. He guided the company safely through the rest of the Second World War and continued to make sure that they maintained their place as one of the leading edge tool manufacturers through the rest of the 1940s.

Post 1950 the company began to find business more difficult. There were an increasing number of suppliers becoming available, particularly from abroad. In 1952 an extensive new catalogue was produced which had a very positive message to both current and past customers.

A group of employees pose for a photograph.

However, the catalogue did not have the desired effect and in September 1955 important changes were made to the "Memorandum of Association". The company struggled on in an ever-changing world. The quality of the product became less

An exhibition stand at a Trade Fair in the 1950s.

important to customers and it became more and more difficult to match the prices of their competitors abroad. Finally, in 1963, the company went into liquidation. The end had come for the family company and the famous "Hedgehog" brand.
Oswald died in 1963 aged 75 and Reginald in 1965 aged 80.

Working a large press at the factory in the 1950s.

Testing to British Standards for hardness during the 1950s.

This is the Handling Room where items are prepared for despatch. It is likely that this is a 1950s photograph.

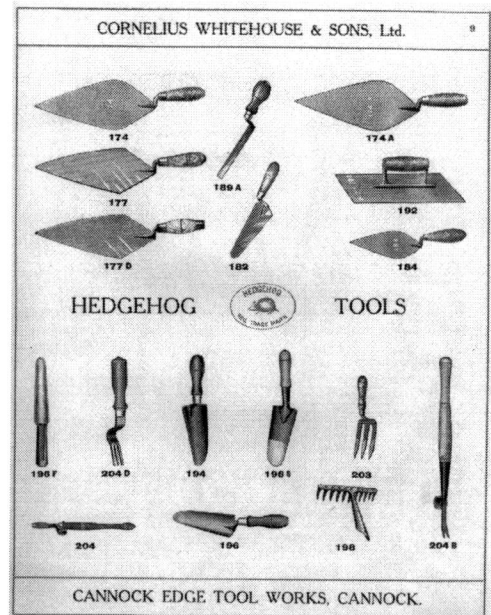

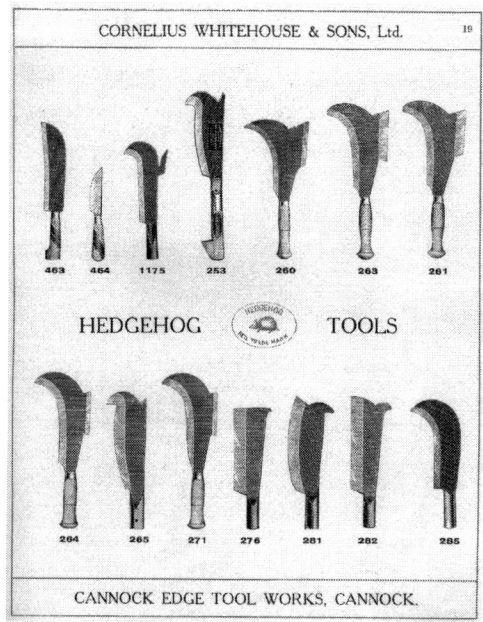

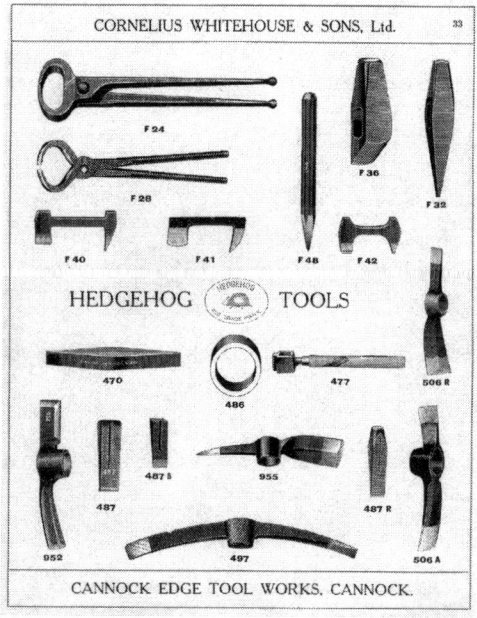

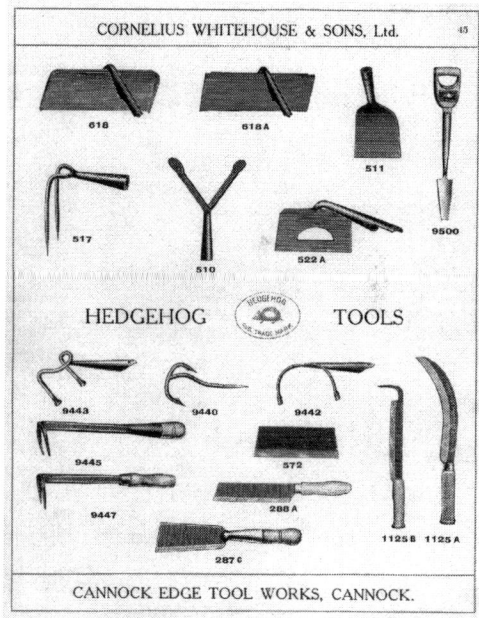

A further four pages taken from the company's 1930 catalogue showing a small selection of their vast product range.

Acknowledgement:
Most of the research for this chapter was carried out by Derrick Middleton.

Chapter Five: **Whitehouse Bros.**

Cornelius and Isaiah Whitehouse had two younger brothers, Job and Henry. Job was only three years younger than Cornelius, being born in 1828 in Wedges Mills. When he left school, he followed his two older brothers into employment at Gilpin's as an edge tool maker. He became a highly skilled employee but was very disillusioned with his role at Gilpin's. Eventually he left Gilpin's and set up an ironmongery shop in Wolverhampton Road, Cannock. However, he still felt unfulfilled and looked for other opportunities.

Job had a younger brother Henry born in 1840 who, like the other boys in the family, began work as an edge tool maker at Gilpin's. Eventually Job and Henry decided to set up a new business for themselves. So it was that, in the 1870s, Whitehouse Brothers came into being. The business manufactured edge tools with Job as the senior partner. Like Cornelius before them, they built their business in Bridgtown. Their new works was built on the junction of North Street and Watling Street and, by 1881, they were employing seventeen men and eight boys.

Job Whitehouse, younger brother of Cornelius, who set up Whitehouse Bros. Ltd. with his younger brother Henry. Judging by the inscription on the photograph this was taken during the days when he ran his own ironmongery business.

These were boom years for the edge tool industry and Job had experience of running a business as well as being a skilled worker himself. Between them the brothers had extensive experience of every department of the edge tool trade and they took extreme care to meet the requirements of their customers. Not surprisingly, the business grew very rapidly both at home and abroad., particularly in Australia and New Zealand.

In the early 1900s the business expanded further to become the only company in the UK to manufacture auger bits of the "Irwin" type. This was done by a completely new process. Within the factory a separate department was created with its own separate steel building, complete with its own motive power and special machinery. All of this was designed and manufactured by the company itself. The auger bits were produced to several specifications. There were "Irwin", "Jennings" and "Solid Nose" patterns, all of which bore the distinctive company name of "Rapid".

After a further few years the company opened a second set of premises called "Atlas Works" at Old Hill in the Black Country. The main purpose of these second premises was to produce the wide range of hammers that the company had successfully produced and marketed worldwide. Henry's son William obtained visas to visit America on two separate occasions between 1900 and 1930. Both of these visits increased the range and sales of these hammers.

The company started in the 1870s. Ten years later they employed 17 men and 8 boys. This photograph shows the size of the workforce early in the twentieth century.

This photograph was taken within the Trip Hammers section of the factory. Working conditions were very basic in those days.

In this photograph blacksmiths use trip hammers to shape the tool blades. Every item was made by a craftsman. No mass production in those days.

Job came to live close to the business at 128 Watling Street but retired early in the century and died on 5th August 1913, aged 85 years. In his will his assets were valued at £8,130 and were divided equally between his daughter and his nephew William Howard Whitehouse.

Here metal is formed into shape on anvils. Conditions inside the factory are extremely hot and sticky but there is a surprising amount of daylight coming from the windows in the roof.

Henry retired soon after his brother Job and left his two sons William and Albert to manage the company. When he died at his home of Heatherleigh, Shoal Hill, Cannock, he left the magnificent sum of £14,334 to his family.

By 1930 the premises had grown so much that they completely dominated a large area on the corner of North Street and Watling Street. But a few years later

William and Albert decided to sell the premises to Mr. E. W. Wynn who converted the premises into a foundry, working with metal on a much larger scale. An amalgamation with Gilpin's was established for the edge tool manufacturing side of the business. Stories abound about how all the equipment and machinery from Whitehouse Bros. was moved on handcarts to Gilpin's premises in Churchbridge.

William Whitehouse moved to the Old Hill Atlas Works where he became Managing Director, That business then changed its name to William Whitehouse & Co. (Atlas Forge) Ltd. The final link with Bridgtown was broken when William's family home on Walsall Road was sold to Bridgtown Social Club as they were in need of larger premises. The Old Hill business continued trading until the 1960s when cheaper imports forced its eventual closure. However, Whitehouse Bros. hammers are now a collectors' item and sell for prices up to £100 each if they are in good condition.

This is the tool sharpening shop. Sandstone was used with water running over the stone to cut down the dust. Many men eventually contracted "Grinders Rot", a breathing condition which shortened their lives.

This was the Handle Fitting Shop. Most of the handles were made at Woottons Timber Yard about 200 yards away in North Street.

Wynn's Corner

There were first-floor premises at Whitehouse Brothers' factory. These premises were later let to a company making dolls. The company concerned was of German origin. They made a variety of dolls, the most famous of which were called Diabolos. As the owners of the factory were German, the premises were "taken over" during World War Two and the company never returned there.

It is surmised that this letting began when the whole premises were taken over by E. W. Wynn. This firm introduced a much heavier form of industry as they were ironfounders. The site became one of the iconic sights and sounds in Bridgtown in that the foundry was noisy, smoky, smelly and very very hot! From that day on all the locals called that spot Wynn's Corner and it is still called that by many people today even though the premises are long gone.

The factory buildings were taken over by E. W. Wynn, Ironfounders during the 1930s. Externally nothing changed with buildings until their eventual demolition.

The new factory was a very different factory from the original edge tool factory of Whitehouse Bros. The overhead cranes and gantries demonstrated many engineering advancements. These can clearly be seen in the photograph on page 50.

The factory caused much consternation in the local community. The soot and the fumes from the factory were cursed by many housewives every Monday which, in those days, was always washday! Washing often had to be fetched back off the washing line to be washed a second time. Local resident Carrie Summers reminisces "Wynn's Foundry blasted out the black sand, as you say, and we had to wipe our window sills every day. When my mother died the post mortem revealed that her lungs were three quarters full of black sand!" The "smogs" in the area were so bad that people sometimes could not even see their own feet. Nevertheless people lived with all these inconveniences as well as the steady thump, thump, thump of the machinery. On the bright side, in cold weather residents could soon get warm by standing in the factory doorway!

Nowadays the site is a very clean and quiet place used for commercial activities.

The photograph shows some casting boxes on the line. The men are holding the wheel of a casting bucket.

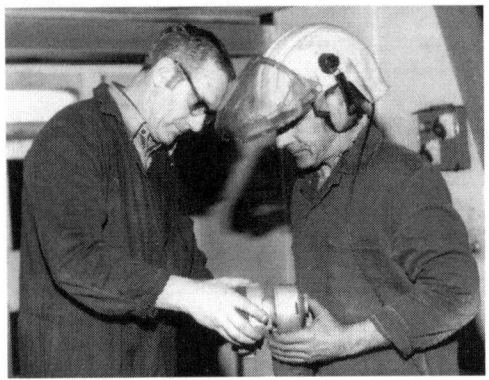

The picture shows the quality checking of a new casting. Now everywhere is much cleaner and more safety precautions are taken.

The premises had stood for over a hundred years but were finally demolished in 1984. This demolition seemed to change the face of Bridgtown forever.

Acknowledgement:
Most of the research for this chapter was carried out by Derrick Middleton.

Chapter Six:
Wood, Tiles, Soap & Manure

This chapter will deal with other industrial trailblazers in the history of Bridgtown.

In the 1851 census Abraham Wootton was a timber merchant operating in Bloxwich. Ten years later he moved his business to Bridgtown to coincide with the development of the new village. He bought some land on the corner of North Street and Walsall Road. The site was known as Brookfield.

This was the spot that everyone knew as "Wootton's Corner". Although it cannot be seen in the picture Wootton's Timber Yard was immediately on the right. Here one of Bridgtown's first ever buses has stopped there. Maybe it was a bus conductor who first coined the name.

Trunks of trees were cut by hand. The saws were long and two-handled with one man at each end, one of them standing in the saw pit. This was a very slow job. Further land was purchased on the corner of North Street and Park Street and a steam powered sawmill was built there. It was the early 1880s and Abraham's two sons, Abraham and Asher, came to run the business, which then became known as A. Wootton & Sons Ltd. The sons had been living in Featherstone. A large chimney stack, about seventy feet high, was built on the new site and this was where the timber was now cut. Once the timber had been cut it was taken across North Street to the Brookfield site where it was left to dry out.

Initially the tree trunks were brought in on horse-drawn wagons called druggens. A later development saw the introduction of Centinal steam wagons and these remained in service until after World War Two. At that point ex-Army lorries were purchased in their place.

Woottons employed their own tree fellers, who would clear trees of all branches before transporting the trunks back to North Street.

Once timber had been cut it was stacked in the yard on the Brookside site to season. There were spacers between the planks to allow air to circulate.

This is one of the powerful Centinal steam wagons used by A. Wootton & Sons Ltd. for transporting heavy loads.

The two Wootton brothers built for themselves two large houses on the Brookfield site, one was called Brookfield and the other The Woodlands. Both of these properties are still in existence today, one as a restaurant and one as a social club.

Asher died in 1899 and Abraham soon afterwards in 1900. Asher's family left the area. One of his sons went to live in America. The other son moved to the south of England and worked as a book-keeper, while his daughter moved elsewhere in Staffordshire. Asher's widow remarried and went to live in Sutton Coldfield.

It was Abraham's family who took over the business. His son Charles took over as managing director, but in 1903 it was Charles's son Cyril who became the last Wootton to be in charge.

This wheelbarrow is another example of the company's craftsmanship. Above a fine set of gates made by A. Wootton & Sons Ltd.

This fine pair of Lych Gates stand at Gentleshaw Church. They were made and presented by one of the two Wootton brothers in memory of his deceased wife.

In 1934 Blencow's Brewery closed in Hollies Avenue, Cannock. Cyril Wootton saw that as a much more suitable premises for his business and so the company moved there, only being about one mile away. The Bridgtown steam mill was closed and demolished. That land was then purchased by the local council who built houses upon it. The Brookfield site was however retained by the company as a suitable place to store large tree trunks until they were ready to be cut. This arrangement lasted until the early 1950s when all company business moved to the Hollies Avenue site. About ten years after that all Wootton involvement ceased with the sale of the company going to Rudders and Paynes of Leamington Spa. That Cannock site now belongs to The Linford Group.

At the new site the company also had a drying kiln in order to speed up the seasoning process. They used sawdust and offcuts to fuel the kiln.

Once the company had relocated to Hollies Avenue in Cannock they had a lot more ground on which to leave the timber to season.

Meanwhile Oliver Wood, who had earlier purchased the Brookfield House as his family home, also purchased the rest of the site, setting down his own tennis court and space for his business of J. Wood & Son. The Woodlands had originally been sold to Handel Whitehouse (see Chapter Four). Meanwhile the area around that junction is still called "Wootton's Corner" by locals as it had since the early days of the village.

Although Bridgtown originally developed around the edge tool industries and coal mining, another industry grew out of that situation. That industry was tile making. Two notable local firms were established, Hawkins Tiles and Rosemary Tiles.

The story of Henry Hawkins making bricks and tiles started on land in Cheslyn Hay. Henry was the son of Joseph Hawkins who appeared in Chapter Three. The Gilpin family had originally made their own bricks and tiles before selling this aspect of their company to Henry Hawkins. After running the business for a while Henry realised that he needed a better supply of clay for his products.

At this time there were two small brickworks alongside Watling Street. In Chapter Three mention was made of the short-lived Waterloo Colliery owned by Lord Hatherton. One of the brickworks was next to the colliery and was called the Old Bog brick-kiln. Very close to it was the Longhouse brick-kiln, also referred to in Chapter Three. Henry was able to rent these brickworks from Lord Hatherton as he knew that a good quality marl had been discovered during the quest for a workable coal seam. Eventually, in 1897, a sale for the mining of clay on an eleven acre site was agreed.

Large steam wagons were used to transport the tiles, all of which had to be loaded by hand. The weight on the lorry was tremendous. Behind the lorry, alongside Watling Street, can be seen a feature that was unique to Hawkins Tileries. There is a series of little structures built to demonstrate the ranges of different tiles available, giving customers a clear view of what they would look like on a roof.

Henry closed down the Cheslyn Hay site and transferred all machinery to the Longhouse site and clay was mined there. Gradually a quarry, known as a "marl hole" locally, formed and this was well-known to all Bridgtonians. In 1947 this "marl hole" was worked out and a new one begun at Redhurst Wood a few miles away.

When Henry died his two sons, Arnold Seymour Hawkins and Leslie C Hawkins became joint managing directors of the company. They employed not only skilled tile manufacturers but clay sculptors too. This was illustrated by the advertising wall that stood by the main road for many years. Sadly, that wall was later demolished by developers.

In the early days all the machinery was driven by steam engines which required the stoking of the fires twenty four hours a day.

There was much machinery to be driven at the tileries and this needed to be done in the times well before electricity was generally available. The machinery was driven by steam engines. Here two tired gentlemen are resting between the hard work of shovelling all that coke into the boilers, but Henry Hawkins Ltd. was also a very innovative company. They developed new methods of production such as hopper-fed screw furnaces which greatly reduced the manpower required for continual stoking, which had been a 24-hours a day job when firing was underway.

Something that is easily forgotten these days is that most of the heavy work was done by horsepower. The picture shows Thomas Matthew Bowdler of Union Street who was a farrier at Hawkins Colliery in the 1930s. His job was to look after the horses which pulled the wagons loaded with clay or with the finished tiles. The horses' feet took a lot of the strain and the farrier it was who cared for them and saw that they were shoed properly.

During World War Two the company went over to the production of munitions. Shell cases were machined and taken to the kiln areas where they were packed with explosives. There was a constant danger of explosion which is why the kiln areas were used. An explosion in a large area would have been devastating. The women who did this job worked twelve hour shifts with one day off a week.

After the war the company quickly reverted to its original business as there

In the early part of the twentieth century a lot of heavy work was done by horses. Here the company's farrier Thomas Bowdler is seen with one of the horses in the 1930s.

Here are two of the lady munitions workers during World War Two. They are in uniform ready for their long tiring shift.

was a significantly high demand for bricks and tiles. There was a lot of building repair work to be done following bomb damage and there was a great need for new houses to be built.

Once the tiles had been made and shaped, they were called green tiles. The photograph below shows women sorting and checking these green tiles in preparation for their transfer to the kilns. The other photograph was taken in 1948. It shows the setters, whose job it was to carry the small bundles of green tiles and stack them systematically in the kilns so that they baked evenly once the kiln was fired.

Women sorting the "green" tiles before they are transferred to the kilns.

Like many other industries the world changed for Hawkins Tiles during the 1950s and the 1960s. Demand for their products decreased, competition increased and the costs of fuel became a constant concern. In June 1957 Arnold Hawkins died but the company struggled on until the death of Leslie Hawkins in March 1985. The company was sold to Tarmac, one of the country's leading construction firms.

Stacking the tiles systematically in the kilns had to be done carefully to ensure that they were baked evenly.

Here is Mr Leslie Hawkins walking across the company yard at about the time when he took over a managing director.

Here is a yard view across Rosemary Tileries. Some time late the company made a marketing stunt of the demolition of the large chimney stack. TV personality Fred Dibnah specialised in such events and large crowds gathered to watch the occasion.

Rosemary Tileries was just over the Bridgtown boundary on the way to Cheslyn Hay but very many of its employees lived in Bridgtown. In fact, the company eventually came to own a number of houses in the village so that they could rent them out to their employees.

1837 was not only the year in which Queen Victoria came to the throne and the year when a first steamship crossed the Atlantic Ocean, it was the year when George Lewis opened up his roofing tile business. Staffordshire is noted for its seams of Etruria marl which appear locally. In addition, the large local supplies of coal were also a major factor in why the Bridgtown area was ideal for this industry. In that year there were more than twenty coalmines nearby.

George Lewis was so proud of the quality of tiles produced that he decided he would name his company after his daughter Rosemary. Local people took up his idea happily and started to refer to the region around the works as Rosemary too. The company's growth and development very much matched that of Henry Hawkins Ltd., even to the fact that it became a munitions factory during World War Two. Its demise also came almost at the same time, as it was taken over by Redland in 1985, ensuring that their product continued to be produced.

Photographs within Rosemary Tiles would be similar to those at Henry Hawkins Ltd. Here instead is a view of packaged tiles stored outdoors.

No photographic evidence has yet been discovered about the soapery described on page 62, or indeed about the Cannock Agricultural Company that succeeded it. Shown in this photograph of the 1919 Victory Celebrations are the cottages that were attached to the company premises.

Way before Bridgtown existed there was a small factory in the area. It was listed as being near to Watling Street. As Bridgtown didn't exist its address was simply given as Cannock. It has now been confirmed that the small business was in fact a soapery. Evidence has been found of references made to it by Haydn Whitehouse no less. An undated newspaper cutting also refers to the finding of a bar of soap bearing the words "The Cannock Toilet Soap" on the one side. On the other side were the words "The Cannock Soapery Company, near Walsall". The journalist writing the press cutting made enquiries at the company called The Cannock Agricultural Company. These enquiries confirmed the fact that their premises in Walkmill Lane had been purchased from the Cannock Soapery Company in 1860.

Some of the ingredients of soap are also used in fertilisers and this might account for the change of use of these premises.

The Patent Urban Manure Company was formed in 1860 for the purpose of making a simple but very effective fertiliser which could easily be applied to the fields. The company needed a site near to a canal as large amounts of sulphuric acid were needed in order to carry out the process. The site in Walkmill Lane suited the company's needs perfectly but there was a small soap manufacturer on that site. The soap factory, called Bancroft & Co, was duly purchased. The manufacture of soap was allowed to continue but a new factory was built alongside.

On the upper floor of the new factory there were large lead-lined vats into which large amounts of animal bones were placed. The vats were then filled with acid, which was left to digest for a period of time. The resultant products were tallow for the soap works, size for glue manufacture and digested bones. The bones were dried out and taken down to the ground floor. They went into a machine called the disintegrator which ground them down to a fine meal. This meal was wheeled in barrows up a ramp to the roof space, taken along some planks before being tipped into 300 ton storage bins below.

The process described above was invented by a German chemist by the name of Von Leibig and the resultant fertiliser is known as phosphate. (Von Leibig is famous as the inventor of Marmite.) Another form of fertiliser was invented in 1842 by a farmer and this was called superphosphate. This replaced animal bones with a fossilised organic substance, initially mined near Cambridge but later imported from Morocco. When the factory was fully functional the plant comprised a Cornish boiler, a 120 feet chimney stack, a steam engine, two bone-digesters and a bone grinding mill. The phosphate dust, together with sulphuric acid, was fed into horizontal tanks. Mixing and cooling then took place before being dug out by hand by men stripped to the waist. It was warm work. These were the men who wheeled the phosphate away into the large storage bins. Later this superphosphate was mixed with other materials according to a secret formula. This was all ground into a friable powder and then packed into hessian sacks.

Soon after the formation of this company they employed a young man by the name of Henry Hart as a clerk. He was to rise very quickly through the ranks and became manager of the works. Henry had a passion for farming and, in particular, for breeding Shire horses. He went on to purchase the Longhouse Farm and he developed a stud farm there, providing both loose boxes and stables in the process. He also built a row of cottages in Walkmill Lane for the workforce, where a blacksmith's shop also came into being. The blacksmith worked for the general public as well as looking after the factory horses and the Shire horses.

The premises of "Cannock Agricultural" were near to the new village of Bridgtown and issued a very potent smell which reached the village when the wind was in the right direction. The villagers had their own name for the company's premises. They called it "The Monkey Muck". Nevertheless the company was a very successful one and regularly supplied businesses all round the country, including many famous sports venues such as Lord's Cricket Ground.

The companies described above were the ones that set Bridgtown as an industrial heartland and gave it life. The growth and development of the area continued apace for over a hundred years. Many more industries and commercial businesses were attracted to the area. In the Cannock Chase area it would often be said that *"If you want to buy something you will find it in Bridgtown!"* By and large this was true.

Acknowledgement
The research for this chapter was carried out by Katherine Page, with help from Trevor McFarlane and Cheslyn Hay & District Local History Society.

This aerial photograph of Gilpin's Works was taken in the early twentieth century. The tall chimney stack in the middle of the picture was demolished in 1933.